Creative Gro

Claiming Your Place

7
Complete
Lessons

Adapted for Group Study by Michael C. Mack & Mark A. Taylor

**STANDARD
PUBLISHING**
Cincinnati, Ohio

Creative Groups Guide: Claiming Your Place

Unless otherwise indicated, all Scripture quotations are from the *Holy Bible: New International Version,* Copyright © 1973, 1978, 1984 by International Bible Society. Used by permission of Zondervan Bible Publishers.

The "NIV" and "New International Version" trademarks are registered in the United States Patent Office by International Bible Society. Use of either requires the permission of International Bible Society.

Scripture quotations marked NASB are taken from The New American Standard Bible, © 1960, 1962, 1968, 1971, 1972, 1973, 1975, 1977 by the Lockman Foundation. Used by permission.

Cover design by SchultzWard, Inc.

The Standard Publishing Company, Cincinnati, Ohio.
A division of Standex International Corporation.

01 00 99 98 97 96 95 94   5 4 3 2 1

ISBN 0-7847-0285-3

Contents

Foreword

Claiming Your Place is about positioning. Your place is vitally important. Your personal growth and satisfaction is directly connected to being in the right place, the position God wants you to occupy. Finding your place is also vital to your congregation. You have an important role to play in the growth of your church. You are a vital contributor. Properly positioned, you help your church to grow. Paul says the body "grows and builds itself up in love, as each part does its work" (Ephesians 4:16).

As if in a giant chess match, too many people have been checkmated in life because they did not find the right position and make the right moves. Happily, no one has to be checkmated at church.

You won't find any X's or O's on the pages that follow. And you'll find no chalkboard. To find your place, you must use the biblical and practical principles that follow to write your own playbook. That lifetime journey of discovery is part of the joy of *Claiming Your Place* in the life of the church.

—Jeffrey A. Metzger

Introduction

Welcome to Creative Groups Guides!

This guide is designed to help the class teacher or group facilitator lead a study of important issues facing adults today. Whether your group meets in a classroom at the church building or in the family room in someone's home, this guide will help you get the most out of your session.

This Creative Groups Guide can be used with or without *Claiming Your Place,* the book compiled and edited by Jeffrey A. Metzger. Use this guide even if you haven't read that book. But if you do read it, you'll be even more equipped for leading the group.

Each section in this guide includes two plans—one for classes and one for small groups. This gives the leader several options:

- •Use the plan just as it is written. If you teach an adult Sunday school or an elective class, use Plan One. If you lead a small group, use Plan Two.

- •Perhaps you teach a Sunday school class that prefers a small group style of teaching. Use the discussion questions and activities in Plan Two, but don't overlook the great ideas presented in Plan One. Mix and match the two plans to suit your class.

- •Use the best of both plans. Perhaps you could start off your class with a discussion activity in Plan Two, and then use the Bible-study section in Plan One. Use the accountability, worship, or memory verse options presented in Plan Two in your Sunday school class. Use some of the "Sunday school" activities and re- source sheets presented in Plan One in your small group meet- ing. Variety is the spice of life!

Resource sheets in each session are available for you to tear out and photocopy for your class or group. Overhead transparency mas- ters are also included for most sessions. Use your own creativity as you decide how to make these resources work for you.

This guide is meant to help you do several things. First, you'll be able to facilitate *active* and *interactive* learning. These methods help students remember and put into practice what they learn. Second, you'll help your class or group *apply* the lessons. These sessions will help your group members actually do something with what they're studying. Third, we've given you lots of *options*. Only you know what will work best in your class or group. Finally, *support and encouragement* are integrated into each session. Learning and application happen best when participants are helping one another. That may mean accountability if your group has built up the trust and caring it takes, or it may simply mean that people are lovingly encouraging one another to continue growing in knowledge and action.

How to Use This Guide

Each session begins with an excerpt from *Claiming Your Place.* This excerpt summarizes the session at a glance. Use it in your preparation or read it to your class or group as an introduction to a session. The central theme and lesson aims will help you understand the main ideas being presented and what outcomes you are looking for. Also, if you want to study the topic further, you can read the chapters listed.

Materials that you will need to have on hand to conduct your session are listed on the first page of each of the plans. Depending on which options in the plans you choose, you may not need all of these materials.

In both the class and group plans, there are three main parts to each session: *Building Community,* a warm-up activity or icebreaker question; *Considering Scripture,* Bible-study activities and discussion; and *Claiming Your Place,* activities or discussion that will help participants apply what they have learned.

In Plan One for Classes, the names of activities are listed in the margins, along with the suggested time for each one. Use these times as you plan your lesson and as you teach to stay on track. In some cases, optional activities are listed. Use these instead of or in addition to other activities as time allows.

In Plan Two for Groups, *italicized type* indicates that this is an instruction for the leader. Plain type indicates a question for the leader to ask or a statement to read. Options for accountability partners are included in the group plans. Use these options to help the group support, encourage, and hold one another accountable. This may not work for a new group, but it will help a group in which trust has already been gained between participants. Other options include worship ideas and a memory verse. Use these at your discretion to help your group grow in love, devotion, and praise for God and for hiding his Word in their hearts.

Use this guide to help you prepare, but we suggest that you do not take this book to your class or group meeting and merely read from it. Instead, take notes on a separate sheet of paper and use that as you lead your group.

As a class teacher or small group leader, you have found at least one place of ministry in Christ's church. An important part of that ministry is helping others mature in their faith and find areas to use their gifts to serve. As you lead others, may you also continue to claim places of ministry and carry them out with passion.

One

Claiming a Place of Faith

*T*he centurion trusted that Christ had power and authority over disease. Consequently, the blessing was his. His faith allowed God to act.

Faith raises our expectations of God. It conquers our antisupernatural bias. Do you expect God to do anything supernatural in your life? Faith admits that God can act in ways we cannot explain.

Sometimes we look at people in the Bible and think, *I could never be like him. I could never be like Paul. What an apostle. I'll never have a place in the church like that. I could never be like Luke, a Gospel writer. I could never be like Peter, a great preacher. They were supermen!*

But take a long, hard look at a lieutenant in the ancient Roman army. He was no Superman. We don't even know his name. Nothing special about him. Just a soldier. He was ordinary in every way until the day he became extraordinary—by faith!

Claiming your place in the church begins at the point of finding your faith. Faith enabled a most unlikely person to find his place in ancient Israel. By faith a centurion found his place in God's kingdom. By faith you can too.
—Jeff Metzger, *Claiming Your Place*

Central Theme:	The first step toward finding our place in the church is demonstrating the kind of faith that the centurion had (Luke 17).
Lesson Aim:	Students will examine an example of faith and attacks on faith to determine whether they have the kind of faith that will lead them to find their places in the church.
Bible Background:	Matthew 13:1-9, 18-23; Luke 7:1-10
For Further Study:	Read Introduction, Foreword, and Chapter One of *Claiming Your Place*.

PLAN ONE  **Classes**

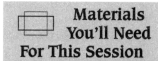

**Materials
You'll Need
For This Session**

Poster board, markers,
pens or pencils, Resource
Sheets 1A–1D

BUILDING COMMUNITY

Distribute copies of <u>Resource Sheet 1A</u> to the class. Ask class members to check the sentences that they feel apply to them. Then read the sentences aloud and ask for those who checked each one to raise their hands. **Tell the class that each of these is a typical sentiment. There are thousands of church members across the country who could identify with each one of them. That's why we need a study like this one. It will help them eliminate the isolation that so many church members feel. It will help them "claim their places" in your local congregation!**

Check the Sentence
5 Minutes

Display the titles of each lesson in this study on a different poster, which you've mounted around the room. (Save these, after this session, to use again with the final discussion in this series.) If you have time, after the above discussion, point members to these titles and ask them to decide . . .

. . . Which seems most appealing to you?
. . . Which do you think you'd most like to discuss?
. . . Which raises the most questions in your mind?
Tell them that you'll look at each of these ideas in this study. Each one will give them another clue about how to find where they fit in the local church.

OPTION
Course Overview
8–10 Minutes

Read the following quote, from the title page of the first chapter in *Claiming Your Place:* "Take care what you believe to be true, for through your belief your reality is formed—Marilee Zdenek" (If you wish, write the quote on the chalkboard so the class can see it.) Discuss with your group:
• What do you think this quote means?
• Has your life ever come to match what you initially believed it would be?
• Our study is about claiming your place in the life of a growing congregation: What reality would you like to see formed regarding your place in a dynamic congregation? What does that look like to you?

Consider the Quote
5 Minutes

Character Study
10 Minutes

CONSIDERING SCRIPTURE

Distribute <u>Resource Sheet 1B</u> to your group. Under the heading, "A Question of Character," group members can jot down their conclusions about several of the character traits of the centurion whose story is told in Luke 7:1-10. Read the text aloud to your class. Then **divide them into pairs, or groups of between five and eight, to complete this section of the Resource Sheet.** After five minutes, ask volunteers to share what they've written under each point. Discuss with your group: **"How does each of these attributes create a place in a person's heart where faith can flourish?"**

The following quotes from Jeff Metzger in *Claiming Your Place* will help you prepare for this discussion:

Humility

An amazing absence of pride is evident in the faith of this Roman. We see no swagger. No puffed chest. No demand that Jesus make an appearance at his premises. Rather, we see an admission of unworthiness and great need. He was much more concerned with others than himself. . . .

Faith cannot flourish in an attitude of arrogant, independent pride. James said it this way, "God opposes the proud but gives grace to the humble. Submit yourselves, then, to God. . . . Come near to God and he will come near to you" (James 4:6-8).

Generous Service

I've been to Capernaum, and I've seen the partially restored ruins of the second-century synagogue built on first-century foundations supplied by the centurion. It is amazing to see the remains of the fine facility built and financed by a generous Roman.

How much do you think it cost to build a synagogue? I have no idea, but I'm sure the cost and effort were significant. It was an extremely generous gift. The centurion lived a giving, not a grasping, life.

Love

The centurion valued people greatly. Notice that this episode is not about the Roman's son or some significant family member. His concern is for his servant. In fact, the word in verse 2 describing the sick individual literally means "slave."

The sick man in this story is property! He is owned by the centurion. Some estimate there were six million slaves in the first century. The slavery of this sick man is not remarkable. The concern of his master is. By Roman law a slave was defined as a living tool. A sick slave could be put to death or discarded without penalty. A human life could be tossed aside as casually as a broken machine.

One Roman writer, commenting about estate management, recommended examining both implements and slaves every year. Those that were old or broken were to be thrown out.

Submission

The centurion clearly understood and submitted to authority. He stated that fact to Jesus: "But say the word, and my servant will be healed. For I myself am a man under authority" (Luke 7:7, 8). He understood both authority and submission from his own experience. He realized that Jesus had resources and authority beyond his own. He was willing to submit to that authority. This attitude is key to faith, and Jesus marveled at its presence in the Roman. . . .

How strong are you on your own? The centurion realized he had no power to handle the situation he faced, but Jesus did. How wise! He submitted to God and sought his strength. "Say the word and my servant will be healed." When will we realize that our resources can include the Father's resources? When will we learn to submit to his authority?

Community

One other element provided an atmosphere for the centurion's faith to grow. He had friends. He was connected to the faith community. The Jewish elders acted on his behalf. Other friends were keeping him posted on the progress of the request and told him of Jesus' approach. Luke 7:6 reports that the centurion sent these friends with his remarkable request for Jesus not to bother entering his house.

This man was wise in being closely connected with other people of faith. Faith rarely grows or flourishes in isolation. Claiming our place of faith means finding our place among people of faith. And surely the example of the faithful centurion had a tremendous impact on his friends.

List the Enemies
10 Minutes

Using the same study groups that formed above, your members can look at Matthew 13:1–9, 19–23. Distribute Resource Sheet 1C.

Give members about five minutes to complete the chart. Then discuss with your whole group. Metzger points out that Satan's attacks are both external and internal. "Trouble and hard times attack faith," he writes in *Claiming Your Place*. "Some receive the seeds of faith with joy, but lacking character in their lives, their faith withers when the heat is on. If our life lacks depth, the seeds of faith will not grow deep roots. When the pressure is on, your faith will quickly fade (Matthew 13:20, 21)."

Other attacks are internal: worry, fear, and bad attitudes. "Be aware," Metzger comments. "You have an enemy who will do everything in his power to hinder the development of dynamic faith in your life."

OPTION
Half and Half
15 Minutes

If you wish to look at both of these passages, but you want to save some time, let half of the class look at the Luke 7 account while the other half studies the parable in Matthew 13. After several minutes, let the groups report as you look at both Scriptures with your whole group.

CLAIMING YOUR PLACE

Discuss the Meaning
10 Minutes

Point members again at the list of centurion's character attributes. Discuss:
1. Which is least present in our current world?
2. Which does the most to cultivate faith in the person who possesses it?
3. If you were to choose one that you need more of, which would you choose?

Next look again at the list of attacks on faith that members found in Matthew 13. Discuss:
1. Which of these attacks have you seen happening in lives of other Christians?
2. Which have you experienced yourself?
3. How does strong faith ward off each kind of attack?
4. How did your faith help you when you felt the devil's attacks?

Read and React
6 Minutes

Distribute Resource Sheet 1D, with its quote by Jeff Metzger from *Claiming Your Place.*

Challenge class members to jot down their answers to these questions, which are printed at the bottom of the sheet:

How do the above paragraphs make you feel? (Be as honest as possible.)

What could you do to broaden your horizons?

Tell your group, **"It's possible that the place God has for you in his church is someplace you never would have imagined—someplace new, challenging, difficult. What can you do now to get ready for the place you may find later?"**

Read the excerpt from the introduction to this lesson (p. 7) before closing with prayer.

PLAN TWO roups

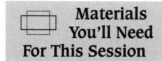

Materials You'll Need For This Session

Resource Sheet 1B (optional) and 1D

PREMEETING

Tape slips of paper with the following phrases from Romans 12:7, 8 onto the chairs in which the group will be sitting: Serving, Teaching, Encouraging, Contributing to the Needs of Others, Leading, Showing Mercy. If you have more than six people in the group, either use some of the phrases twice or come up with additional gifts and abilities. As the group arrives and begins to get settled, tell them to find the place they think applies to them best. Allow them to help one another decide. After everyone has found a place, explain the purpose of this seven-week course: to help us identify and claim our individual places in Christ's church.

BUILDING COMMUNITY

If you had no barriers of time and money, what's one thing you'd like to help make happen in our congregation (or in the church universal)?

CONSIDERING SCRIPTURE

Read Luke 7:1-10

1. What are some of the centurion's character traits? *(Refer to Resource Sheet 1B or distribute copies of it to your group after they've listed several themselves.)*

2. *Discuss each character trait separately. If there are ten or more people in the group, write the following questions on note cards and have them work in pairs on one of these traits. Then have them share their findings with the entire group. (Use the commentary on pages 10 and 11 for help guiding the discussion.)*
• ***Humility***
   Which verses show the centurion's humility?
   How does humility help one's faith to flourish?
• ***Service***
   Which verses show the centurion's willingness to serve others?
   How do service and generosity help one's faith to flourish?

OPTION
Accountability Partners

Ask group members to find a partner to meet or talk with on the phone throughout this series. This week, ask them to discuss areas of strength and weakness in their faith, and what steps they can take to allow their faith to flourish.

OPTION
Worship Ideas

• Ask several people to read some or all of these sections from Hebrews: 11:1, 2; 5, 6; 7; 8–10; 11, 12; 24–28; 30; 12:1–3. Then close in prayer, thanking God for these faithful witnesses and asking for group members' faith to flourish.

• Song suggestions
"He Is Lord,"
arranged by Tom Fettke
"The Greatest Thing,"
by Mark Pendergrass
"Have Thine Own Way, Lord,"
by Adelaide A. Pollard

OPTION
Memory Verse

"And without faith it is impossible to please God, because anyone who comes to him must believe that he exists and that he rewards those who earnestly seek him" (Hebrews 11:6).

• *Love*
Which verses show the centurion's love?
What does it mean to "value someone highly"?
How does love help one's faith to flourish?

• *Submission*
Which verses show the centurion's submission?
How can asking God for something be an act of submission?
How does submitting to God help one's faith to flourish?

• *Community*
In what sense was the centurion connected to a faith community?
Faith cannot flourish in isolation. Do you agree or disagree? Why?
How can this group help your faith to flourish?

3. Of the character traits we've just discussed, which do you think is most essential in your area of ministry or the service you'd like to be involved in?

4. In verse 6, the centurion calls Jesus "Lord." What does it mean to call Jesus "Lord"?

5. What potential barriers were present to keep the centurion from demonstrating faith in Jesus?

6. How does faith break down barriers built by bigotry?

7. How can breaking down these barriers help the church to reach and serve the world?

CLAIMING YOUR PLACE

1. *Read the quote from Resource Sheet 1D. Then ask,* Why did Paul and Abraham leave perfectly good and safe positions to enter the unknown?

2. Do you know of anyone who has demonstrated extraordinary faith by going, yet not knowing?

3. *Option: Read the excerpt from the title page of this session.*

4. Do you expect God to do anything supernatural in your life?

5. What steps will you take this week to allow your faith to flourish? *(Refer back to the character traits, discussed earlier.)*

6. How can we help each other's faith to flourish?

Check the Sentence
that applies to you

☐ 1. I'd like to do something important for God, but I don't know where to start.

☐ 2. I feel guilty when I say no to a request for help, even if it's something I know I wouldn't do well.

☐ 3. The workers at this church all seem to be longtime members. How does a newcomer like me fit in?

☐ 4. If I could change something about myself to help my congregation grow, I would probably do it.

☐ 5. It's hard for me to see the connection between my Christian life and my congregation's growth.

A Question of Character

Someone has said that character is what we do when no one is looking. The impressive thing about this centurion is that he wasn't out to impress anyone (Luke 7:1-10). He was simply being himself. The centurion's character was right for faith to grow. Several attributes of his character are obvious in this passage.

—Jeff Metzger, Claiming Your Place

First read the Bible account. Then look at this list of attributes and decide how the centurion in this passage demonstrates each one.

Humility (Notice especially verses 6 & 7)

Generous Service (Note especially verse 5)

Love (Note especially verse 2)

Submission (Note especially verse 7 & 8)

Community (Note especially verse 6)

A Question of
FAITH

When faith flourishes, Satan is unhappy. He will throw all his energy into stealing the faith of believers like us. Christ explains this in the parable recorded in Matthew 13. Read Matthew 13:1-9, 19-23, and then complete the chart below.

Types of soil	What each represents	How does the devil attack faith rooted in this kind of soil?

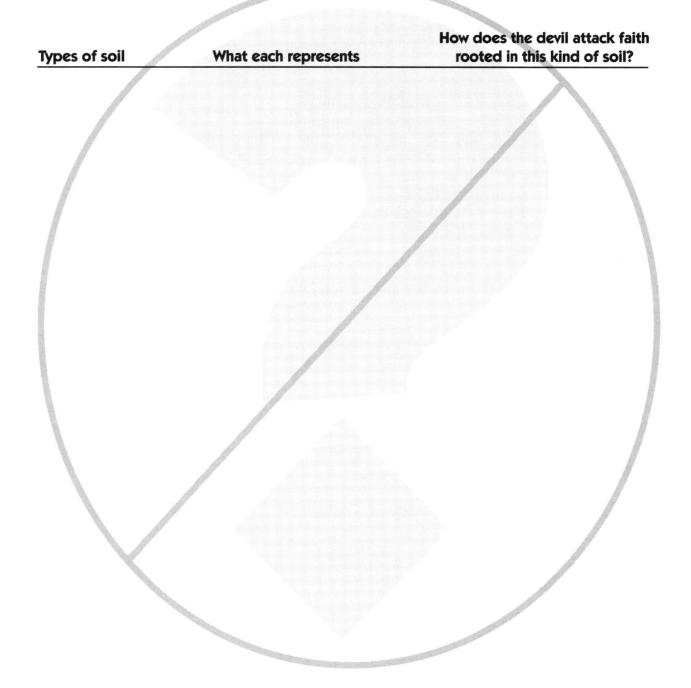

Cultivate
Your Character

WHAT ARE YOU DOING to cultivate your character and strengthen your faith? The place to begin building your faith is at the point of your character.

Character building occurs when horizons are broadened. The centurion was far from home, not a native of Capernaum. He had been posted there. It was his duty. He was a foreigner who was out of his element. But he chose to bloom where he was planted. Rather than being discouraged by his distance from his roots, he grew new ones. He deepened his perspective and looked for God.

There is a biblical principle of faith worth noting in this example. Faith is not acquired by vegetating in one little corner for a lifetime. Sometimes we value our security too highly. But the ultimate goal of life is not earthly security. Our goal is to grow until we become like Christ.

I'm going, not knowing. This theme recurs throughout Scripture. Paul stated it standing on a beach at Miletus. With tears in his eyes he said, "I am going to Jerusalem, not knowing what will happen to me there" (Acts 20:22).

Hebrews 11:8 makes a similar statement about Abraham: "By faith Abraham, when he was called . . . obeyed and went, even though he did not know where he was going."

Sometimes faith demands that we leave the safe, the secure, and the known to enter the unknown. Why did these people of faith leave perfectly good and safe positions to enter the unknown? Why did they step right off the end of the dock and onto faith footing? Why were they going, yet not knowing? They were prompted by the Lord himself. . . .

Faith sometimes requires that we go, that we move beyond our horizon, not knowing what will be the result except that we go with God.

Faith requires a willingness to say yes when God says "Go."

—Jeff Metzger, *Claiming Your Place*

1. How do the above paragraphs make you feel? (Be as honest as possible.)

2. What could you do to broaden your horizons?

Two

Claiming a Place of Serving Others

*T*he blessings of a ministering church are endless. Consider the positive benefits that come naturally as the church develops a heart for ministry. Assimilation of new members into the church is a direct result of a ministry emphasis. The instruction in new-members classes, the gift analysis offered in new-member orientation, the pulpit and classroom emphasis on every-member ministry builds into new members the biblical expectation that they, too, should use their spiritual gifts to serve others and claim their place in the church. Getting involved becomes a natural process and the tradition of your congregation.

Fellowship is enhanced as individuals who have identified their gifts combine them with others on a ministry team and serve the Lord, his church, and their community together in the small group. The most effective means of conserving people is to get them connected and involved in ministry.

Our God "is able to do immeasurably more than all we ask or imagine, according to his power that is at work within us" (Ephesians 3:20). When relatively few people are solely responsible for the thinking, imagining, and decision making in the church, we limit God's power to work within us. When we decentralize decision making and encourage the whole church to think and imagine, we enlist God's empowering Spirit to work within us.

Ministry is the key to an effective church! No matter how you approach it, ministry brings the blessing of God. Even if we're not 100 percent correct in every way, when we offer what we do to the Lord, he acknowledges our effort.

—Dennis Bratton, *Claiming Your Place*

Central Theme: Finding your place in the life of the church demands a willingness to serve.

Lesson Aim: Students will explore passages about giftedness and express a desire to use their gifts to serve.

Bible Background: Romans 12:4-8; 1 Corinthians 12:12-26; Ephesians 4:11-16

For Further Study: Read Chapter Two of *Claiming Your Place.*

 **Classes**

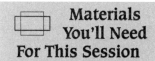
Materials You'll Need For This Session

Resource Sheets 2A and 2B, Transparency Master 2A, pens or pencils

BUILDING COMMUNITY

To begin this session, ask each member to choose a partner. The **pairs** should discuss the following question for two minutes: **"If you had to give up one of your five senses, which one would you choose? Why?"**

If you wish to take the time, let a few tell what they chose, and why. You might want to find one person for each of the five senses (hearing, seeing, smelling, touching, tasting). Then tell your group, **"Today's lesson looks at the Scripture's picture of the church as a body and how individual members of the body must be committed to serving each other. Just as you would hate to give up any part of your body, the body of Christ needs every member in order to do its work effectively. A servant spirit is an important step toward finding your place in the church."**

Neighbor Nudge
5–10 Minutes

CONSIDERING SCRIPTURE

With his chapter in *Claiming Your Place,* Dennis Bratton, minister with a dynamic congregation in Jacksonville, Florida, makes a long list of observations about why the church should be a serving place, and how every congregation can become a place of service. He suggests principles followed by his congregation and proposes that each one is based squarely on a scriptural foundation. **In today's study, class members will first consider several passages that speak about the need for each member of the church to be a servant. Then, if you have time, lead them to read quotes from Bratton's chapter and to decide for each one: "How do these Scriptures support this principle?"**

Members will study Romans 12:4–8; Ephesians 4:11–16; and 1 Corinthians 12:12–26, using the discussion questions on Resource Sheet 2A. You may divide your class into thirds and assign one of the Scriptures to each group. Or, if your class is large, you may form many groups of between five and eight members each. Ask a different volunteer to read each of these passages aloud to the whole group. Then each group chooses one of the Scriptures to discuss.

Scripture Search
15–20 Minutes

Give the groups about ten minutes to discuss their Scriptures. If a group finishes before you call time, it can consider a second passage and its questions. Then discuss these with your whole class.

Read and React
15 Minutes

If you have time, distribute Resource Sheet 2B, containing quotes from Bratton in *Claiming Your Place*. Members are to decide how the Scriptures studied today support each of these principles. **Members should write specific references under each quote, along with an explanation of how the Scripture supports the idea.**

After several minutes, discuss the quotes with your class, letting members explain how they see specific verses supporting each of the paragraphs.

CLAIMING YOUR PLACE

Finish the Sentences and Pray
6–10 Minutes

Display Transparency 2A, which contains these words from 1 Peter 4:10: "Each one should use whatever gift he has received to serve others." Ask class members to complete the following sentences (also on this transparency) on blank sheets of paper:

1. Gifts I could use to serve others include . . .
2. If I could do anything to help the church grow, it would be . . .
3. The area where I need help finding my place is . . .

Perhaps students would be willing to share their answers with others in the class. Use the Bible-study groups already formed, or divide members into pairs within the groups. In pairs, then, or in groups, members pray together to finish this session.

PLAN TWO roups

PREMEETING

Before the meeting, write the following words on individual index cards: **Feet, Hands, Ears, Eyes, Mouth, Shoulders, Elbows, Knees, Heart, Brain.** *If you are artistic, draw the body parts on the cards as well (or cut them from a magazine and paste them on). Have the host or hostess randomly give each person a card as he arrives and tell him to consider what personality traits are associated with this body part. Keep one card for yourself. When everyone has arrived, instruct the group to give their cards to others whose personalities or giftedness are described by that body part. If some members receive more than one card, they are to give all but one to other group members. Keep going until everyone has one card, and then ask them to share what body parts they have. Discuss with the group why they think each person has the card he or she has.*

BUILDING COMMUNITY

If you had to give up one of your five senses, what would it be? Why?

CONSIDERING SCRIPTURE

Ask two people to read 1 Corinthians 12:12–26 and Romans 12:1–8.

Option: If your group has eight or more participants, divide in half. Each group will take one of the passages listed above. Before the meeting, ask your apprentice or assistant leader, or some other capable person, to lead one of the groups. Photocopy or write out the questions below for the other group. After both groups have finished, let each group briefly share their findings with everyone.

1. Can anyone summarize in one sentence what Paul is saying in these passages?

2. Why do you think Paul felt the need to write these things to these two congregations? What do you suppose was going on there?

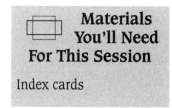

Materials You'll Need For This Session

Index cards

Accountability Partners

Ask partners to meet for a few minutes now (or, if you need the time, during the week) to help one another identify their gifts and encourage each other in using those gifts to serve others. Ask them to talk during the week and continue praying for each other.

Worship Ideas

• Read Psalm 100 together as an act of worship.

• Song suggestions
"In My Life, Lord, Be Glorified," by Bob Kilpatrick
"People of God," by Wayne Watson
"In Christ There Is No East or West," by John Oxenham

Memory Verse

"Just as each of us has one body with many members, and these members do not all have the same function, so in Christ we who are many form one body, and each member belongs to all the others" (Romans 12:4, 5).

---

3. In what ways are Christians different or unique from one another?

4. What do Christians have in common with one another?

5. How does God arrange the parts of the body just as he wants them to be?

6. Paul says the suffering of one part of the human body can make the rest of the body suffer. Can you give an example of this?

7. How might that happen in the church?

8. When have you felt like an important or essential part of the body?

9. What are some specific results of the body of Christ working together?

10. What difference can it make when Christians are more concerned about getting results than getting credit?

CLAIMING YOUR PLACE

1. What do you want to do to serve others?

2. *Discuss again the different gifts that individuals in the group have. Ask,* How can these different gifts that we have work together to bring results in the church and glory to God? *Ask for practical illustrations.*

A *Serving* Place

*A*s we commit ourselves to service, we will find our place in the local church. The church does not exist to entertain us or serve us while we watch it from the outside. Instead, as a living organism, our needs are met as we meet the needs of others in the body of Christ. Read the following Scriptures to see how the New Testament makes this principle clear:

Romans 12:4-8

1. How should a human body compare with the church?
2. What relationship do Christians have with each other? with Christ?
3. What are the gifts Paul includes in his list? What is a Christian supposed to do if he discovers that he has one of these gifts? Circle those gifts that you'd like to study more.
4. Read this passage from several translations. Do the different versions lend insight into how each of these gifts can contribute to the health of the whole body?

Ephesians 4:11-16

1. According to these verses, what should be the function of leaders in the church? (See verse 12.)
2. What happens to the church when God's people are adequately prepared for works of service? How would you describe this result in just one word?
3. Describe the church when members are not being prepared for works of service?
4. What does this passage say about the relationship of Christ to the church and to each of its various members? What part does Christian service play in this relationship? (See verse 16.)

1 Corinthians 12:12-26

1. According to this passage, do individual body members have any choice about whether they are a part of the body? What implication does this have for the Christian's attitude toward the church? toward other individual Christians in the church?
2. How is the eye helped by the ear? How is the ear helped by the nose? How is the head helped by the feet? What does Paul's extended illustration here say about how individuals in the church should function together?
3. Sometimes we wish we had abilities, gifts, or functions that seem always to go to someone else. How does this passage, especially verse 18, help us deal with this problem?
4. We're studying this passage in a lesson about service. What does this Scripture have to do with service?

Adapted from *Claiming Your Place,* edited by Jeffrey A. Metzger, copyright © 1994, The Standard Publishing Company. Permission to reproduce for ministry purposes only.

𝒫rinciples for Today

Each of the following quotes is by Dennis Bratton, from his chapter in *Claiming Your Place.* Consider each of these ideas, and decide how it grows from the scriptural principles we have already discussed in this session. Below each quote write a reference from Romans 12:4–8, Ephesians 4:11–16, or 1 Corinthians 12:12–26 and jot how this quote demonstrates the verse(s).

• The church should not have uninvolved members! Every member has a function. Each of us is an important part of the body of Christ. We're not here for ourselves. We belong to each other. That means we're committed to a common cause. As each of us has different gifts according to the grace given to us, we are to be faithful in the use of those gifts.

• When God's people do their works of service, prepared for that service by church leadership, the results are incredible. Not only is the body built up . . . it reaches unity in the faith, it has a more complete knowledge of the Son of God, and it becomes mature, "attaining to the whole measure of the fullness of Christ." Everyone finds his or her place, and every place is important. A ministering church realizes these important promises fulfilled in its fellowship.

• A ministering church utilizes its staff more effectively. Those called to church leadership have been trained to lead others in ministry. Encouraging staff ministers to be equippers of the saints brings obvious benefits. Preachers can multiply their gifts and the results of their labors by equipping and enabling church members.

• There is no end to the benefits in a ministry-driven church. It is amazing how much can be accomplished when people are concerned with getting results rather than with getting credit. The congregation that learns the lesson of gift-related, servant-hearted, fruit-producing ministry has learned the key to being an effective church.

• A ministering church hears transitional words more readily. Their church becomes my church. What they are doing becomes what I am doing. People who have been mere spectators get involved. Personal ownership is essential when building a dynamic congregation.
Since we began emphasizing every-member ministry, the percentage of our membership involved in gift-related ministry has nearly tripled. When we started doing a better job of helping people discover their unique spiritual gifts, we saw the majority of our members find real joy in serving Jesus. Conversely, we've stopped seeing people burn out in church work.

• Preachers and elders who try to know it all, decide it all, and do it all may be committed leaders, but there's a better way. Leaders who equip, motivate, and mobilize their congregations will have fewer late-night meetings. They will have less stress since everything no longer rests on their shoulders alone. And they will see the amazing things God wants to do through the ministering people they oversee.

"Each one should use whatever gift he has received to serve others"

(1 Peter 4:10).

Complete the following sentences on blank sheets of paper:

1. Gifts I could use to serve others include . . .

2. If I could do anything to help the church grow, it would be . . .

3. The area where I need help finding my place is . . .

Three

Claiming a Place of Bold Witness

*W*hat comes to mind when you think about boldly sharing your faith? Many confuse boldness with being brash or overly blunt. They think of an "in your face, nail 'em to the wall, give 'em hot gospel" kind of witness. But being bold does not mean being rude. Being bold simply means having the courage to share what Christ has done in your life.

Boldness, holy boldness, is an essential attitude for strengthening and presenting your faith. And boldness is a vital element of finding your place and doing your part in a growing church. Our world is filled with tests and challenges.

Life is no place for the timid. Courageous boldness is our need.

—Steven T. Reeves, *Claiming Your Place*

Central Theme:	One place for every Christian is that of a witness. Each of us should consider how to offer a bold witness for Christ.
Lesson Aim:	Group members will discover biblical principles for sharing their testimony, write their own testimony, and commit to sharing their testimony.
Bible Background:	Acts 26; 1 Peter 3:13-16
For Further Study:	Read Chapter Three of *Claiming Your Place*.

Classes

BUILDING COMMUNITY

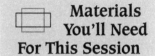

Give each member a slip of yellow, white, blue, or pink paper as they enter the room, so that about one-fourth of the class has each color.

On one of the yellow slips, write: **"Whenever the minister starts talking about witnessing, I feel. . . ."**

On one of the white slips, write: **"The person most influential in leading me to Christ was. . . ."**

On one of the blue slips, write, **"Before I could effectively share my faith in Christ with someone else, I. . . ."**

On one of the pink slips, write: **"I think evangelism is easy/difficult (pick one), because. . . ."**

To begin your session, ask everyone to look at his or her slip to see who has the slips with words on them. These four people are your leaders. **Tell class members to form themselves into groups, according to the color of slip they're holding.** The leader's job is to read the open-ended sentence to his or her group and to ask each person in the circle to complete the sentence.

Give the groups several minutes to discuss among themselves. Then discuss with the class:

1. In your group did you hear mostly positive feelings or mostly negative feelings about the subject of evangelism?

2. Why do Christians sometimes feel guilty when someone talks or teaches about evangelism?

Tell the class that this session should make them feel better about evangelism: more willing and more able to share their faith with the non-Christians they know.

Instead of dividing your members into groups, simply read some or all of the open-ended sentences to the class, or write them on the board. Let members complete the sentences on a slip of paper and then return them to you, without signing their names. Read the answers to the group. Then proceed with the two discussion questions suggested above.

Sentence Slips
10–15 Minutes

> **Materials You'll Need For This Session**
>
> yellow, white, blue, and pink slips of paper; Transparency Master 3A, Resource Sheet 3A, pens or pencils

OPTION
Anonymous Answers
5–10 Minutes

CONSIDERING SCRIPTURE

Ask class members to study 1 Peter 3:13–16 and **make a list of "principles for relating to a lost world"** they can find in this passage. They should do this work in groups of about five. After eight or ten minutes, ask the groups to share with the whole class.

In chapter 3 of *Claiming Your Place,* Steven Reeves suggests the following principles from 1 Peter 3. You may want to display them, using Transparency 3A, and see how many of these the class members discovered on their own.

A Desire for Goodness (v. 13). "To approach life from Jesus' perspective would be to have a desire for goodness," Reeves writes. "In a world of threats and challenges, if you set your sights on being like Christ, the world won't have much success at attacking your testimony."

A Flexibility in Suffering (v. 14). "It is true that people don't usually harm those who want to do good. But if it does happen, remember that you are blessed in the eyes of God. . . . For the Christian there is a certain blessedness in suffering, even in the midst of sorrow. That's what Peter meant when he quoted Isaiah 8:12: 'Do not fear what they fear, and do not dread it.'

"If your relationship with God is most important, you do not need to fear. Be bold. You may suffer, but you will be saved. The key to this kind of courage is the place Jesus has in your heart."

A Place for Christ (v. 15). "So often we emphasize what is on our lips rather than what is in our hearts. We are preoccupied more with what we say than what we are. The non-Christian is not interested in what we have to say until he or she sees what we really are. There is no lasting courage and very little power apart from a personal connection with Christ."

A Readiness to Answer (v. 15). "Some people can communicate the gospel better than others. They do it in a way that people understand and want to believe. But everyone can tell his or her own story. In fact, no one can tell your story as you can. What you have to share is powerful, and it will touch people."

A Winsome Attitude (vv. 15, 16). Reeves points out three attributes of an effective witness:

• *Gentleness.* Reeves challenges his readers to offer "a gentle testimony in brokenheartedness." We are not arrogant with what we share, for we can take no credit for it. We offer to others the hope that has transformed our own lives.

• *Respect.* "We must share the love of God in a loving way. . . .

"Try to understand their [other people's] perspective as you handle the Word. People are precious and important to God. They deserve to be treated that way at all times. Giving respect increases the impact of your witness."

• *Integrity.* Reeves points to verse 16 and says, "Live your life in such a way that your conscience is clear. If you act like a person who has a new life in Christ, the world, with its challenges and threats, will be disarmed."

Class members can turn to Acts 26 and write a summary of Paul's testimony before Festus and Agrippa. Tell them it is an example of the bold witness that we should offer to our world. Give members several minutes to work on this in groups. (Each group prepares one summary.) Then the groups can compare their work as you discuss as a whole class.

Discuss: "How would you characterize Paul's testimony? What words describe it best?"

Reeves points out that Paul, a great intellectual, could have used his reason and knowledge to try to convince these two officials. Instead, he told the story of how Christ confronted him and how he responded. His witness was simple, straightforward, and bold. But it was not complicated, theological, or difficult.

Discuss: "What can we learn about our witness from the example of Paul in this passage?"

If you wish, do both of the above activities. Half of the class can study 1 Peter 3 while the other half studies Acts 25. Then they can share with each other what they've found.

CLAIMING YOUR PLACE

Challenge class members to think about their own testimony. Distribute Resource Sheet 3A, which provides an outline to help them write out their testimony.

Give members about 10 minutes to prepare their written testimonies. Then ask each person to find a partner and to share what he or she has written. They may read if they wish, or they may share as much as possible from their heart. This should not take more than another six minutes.

Challenge members, with their partners, to think of non-Christians with whom they could share their testimony. Partners close with prayers for each other, prayers for boldness to be a witness, and prayers for wisdom as they decide when to share and with whom.

OPTION
Scripture Summary
10–15 Minutes

OPTION
Half and Half
15–25 Minutes

Prepare Your Testimony
20 Minutes

PLAN TWO roups

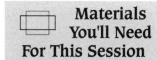 **Materials You'll Need For This Session**

Resource Sheet 3B, index cards, pens or pencils

PREMEETING

As people begin getting settled, hand them Resource Sheet 3B, "Test Your Knowledge About Evangelism," and ask them to complete it. Use this as a discussion starter for the next activity.

BUILDING COMMUNITY

1. How would you define evangelism?

2. *Option: During the week before the meeting, ask a few people from the group whether they would mind sharing (in about five minutes each) how they were led to Christ. Ask them to share now.*

3. *Option: Ask whether anyone would share how they were led to Christ by a friend or how they have led someone else to the Lord.*

4. *Option:* Indicate by a show of hands how you were led to the Lord (you may respond more than once). (a) by a preacher; (b) by walking into a church service and hearing the gospel preached; (c) through Sunday school; (d) through an evangelistic crusade; (e) through a visitation program of a church; (f) through another program of the church; (g) through a special need ministry (such as Alcoholics Anonymous); (h) through a friend or relative.

    Then say, In a poll of Christians, 6 percent were led to Christ by a preacher, 5 percent through the Sunday school, one-half of 1 percent through an evangelistic crusade, 1 percent through a visitation program, 3 percent through another program, 2 percent through a special need, and **79 percent by a friend or relative.**

• What does this tell you about the effectiveness of people versus programs in bringing people to Christ?

CONSIDERING SCRIPTURE

Read 1 Peter 3:13–16

1. How does setting apart Christ as Lord prepare us to be witnesses?

2. In a court of law, what is a witness? How is that like being a Christian witness?

3. One of the spiritual gifts we saw in last week's study was that of an evangelist. What's the difference between being an evangelist and being a witness?

4. Has anyone ever asked you to "give the reason for the hope that you have"?

5. What might prompt a person to ask us about our hope?

6. How can we be bold in our witness and, at the same time, do it with gentleness and respect?

7. *Option: Have several people read the following passages out loud; then discuss the questions below:*

> *John 13:34, 35*
> *Acts 1:7, 8; 2:32, 37–41, 47*
> *2 Corinthians 2:12–17*
> *2 Corinthians 5:11–21*
> *Colossians 4:2–6*

- How do these verses add to your understanding of what a witness is and does?
- What is our part in evangelism as opposed to God's part?
- What does "lifestyle" evangelism mean to you?

CLAIMING YOUR PLACE

Distribute two index cards to each person. Ask participants to write on one of the cards the names of non-Christians they know and would be willing to pray for. Suggest they put at least one name for each of these three areas: at work or school, in their neighborhoods or apartment buildings, in their families. Instruct them to copy the information onto the other card. Ask them to give you one of the cards and keep the other for themselves. If time allows, discuss whose names you've written on the cards. Then put all the cards you've collected onto a plate or into a basket in the middle of the room. Take turns praying for the people who are represented by these cards. Pray for opportunities to develop friendships with them, minister to them, show them God's love, find areas of common ground, and be a bold yet gentle witness in their lives. After praying, tell the group to place their cards where they will remind them throughout each day to pray for these people.

OPTION
Accountability Partners

Have accountability partners meet during the week to practice telling their story to one another. Suggest this format: (1) My life before I met Christ; (2) How I met Christ and came to know him; (3) My life since I met Christ. Also, ask them to hold each other accountable for praying for their non-Christian friends, neighbors, or relatives and to share Christ's love with them.

OPTION
Worship Ideas

- Read Psalm 67 together as an act of worship.

- Song suggestions
"Shine, Jesus Shine," by Graham Kendrick
"Carry the Light," by Twila Paris
"Send the Light," by Charles H. Gabriel

OPTION
Memory Verse

"But in your hearts set apart Christ as Lord. Always be prepared to give an answer to everyone who asks you to give the reason for the hope that you have. But do this with gentleness and respect" (1 Peter 3:15).

My Testimony

➡️ My life before I met Christ

➡️ How I met Christ and came to know him

➡️ My life since I met Christ

Test Your Knowledge About
EVANGELISM

1. You are asked to head your church's evangelism program. How do you respond?
a. Hire a blimp to drop tracts on the freeway during rush hour.
b. Tell them you need to pray about it—for at least a year.
c. Ask if you could serve on the tract-stapling committee instead.
d. Start practicing your Billy Graham imitation.

2. What does lifestyle evangelism mean to you?
a. Going to a restaurant and leaving a tract as a tip.
b. Playing the Christian radio station loudly enough for all your neighbors to hear.
c. Tossing a "Jesus Frisbee" at the beach.
d. Jogging in your "I'm a Jesus-praisin' California raisin" T-shirt.

3. You notice a new neighbor moving in next door. How do you respond?
a. Pretend you don't see him until he's moved everything in.
b. As he's carrying in the piano, say, "Hey, if you were to have a heart attack and die right now, do you know if you'd go to Heaven?"
c. Welcome him, and then suggest that he trim his spruce tree so it doesn't hang over the fence anymore.

4. How should you respond when someone says, "There's something different about you. What is it?
a. "I just shaved off my beard."
b. "What do you mean by 'different,' buster?"

c. "You don't see paisley polyester leisure suits like this one very often, do you?"
d. "I'm a born-again, dispensational, premillenial, Spirit-filled evangelical who's been regenerated, justified, and sanctified by Christ's glorious act of atonement."

5. When you're doing door-to-door evangelism, what's the first thing you should say when someone comes to the door?
a. "Did you know that God loves you, even though you turned the lawn sprinkler on me?"
b. "Could you please remove your dog's teeth from my leg?"
c. "What a lovely home, and what nice end tables you have. Speaking of end, if you were to die tonight . . ."
d. "What a beautiful clock! When your time runs out . . ."

6. A visitor to your church asks, "What does your God have to say about the ontological problem of the ground of Being?" How do you respond?
a. "Say what?"
b. Tell her you don't discuss things like that in public.
c. Check to see if you still have your wallet.
d. Tell her you gave up ontology for Lent.

7. The person sitting next to you on the plane is reading Shirley Maclaine's *Out on a Limb*. What do you say to initiate a conversation?
a. Nothing—you ask the stewardess for another seat.

b. "I'm not getting all the channels on my headphone. Could you help me?"
c. "I see by your aura that you're interested in spiritual things."
d. "If you believe that stuff, why do you need an airplane?"

8. What's the best way to witness to people at work?
a. Anonymously fax gospel tracts to your business contacts.
b. Hold a Bible study during work time—after all, we're commanded to seek first the kingdom of God."
c. Ask the boss if you can open the meetings in prayer.
d. Leave detailed instructions for the person who will take over your job after the rapture.

9. Someone notices you reading the Bible and asks, "Do you really believe that stuff?" You say,
a. "No, I just look at it for the pictures."
b. "No, I'm helping my son do a book report."
c. "Quit bothering me! Can't you see I'm doing a Bible study on evangelism?"

10. You're telling a neighbor that she needs to believe in God, and she responds, "I am God." What do you do?
a. Ask for clarification.
b. Ask for proof.
c. Kneel.
d. Run.

Your score. If you selected any of the alternatives above, you may need to learn more about evangelism.

Principles for Relating to a
Lost World
1 Peter 3:13–16

① **A Desire for Goodness**

② **A Flexibility in Suffering**

③ **A Place for Christ**

④ **A Readiness to Answer**

⑤ **A Winsome Attitude**
- Gentleness
- Respect
- Integrity

Four

Claiming a Place of Passion

*G*od's Word is full of encouragement to personal dedication. The Lord assures me that I am to live for his glory (1 Corinthians 10:31), not my gain or men's approval. It is the call to passion.

When God tells me to love, he tells me to do it fervently (1 Peter 4:8). Friendships are to be maintained devotedly (Romans 12:10). When steering clear of evil, I am told to stay away even from the appearance of it (1 Thessalonians 5:22). Anything less is not 100 percent. When seeing a brother or sister in need, I am to bear his or her burden sacrificially (Galatians 6:1, 2), not stay at a safe distance. When it comes to work, I am to be disciplined and diligent (1 Thessalonians 2:7-9). Again and again God calls me to give the Christian life my all. Half measures will not do for fully devoted followers of Jesus Christ. I am immersed in the pursuit of the power and passion of 100 percent commitment, 100 percent effort.

—Jeff Metzger, *Claiming Your Place*

Central Theme: We will most readily find our place in the church when living for Christ is our first priority.

Lesson Aim: Students will summarize Paul's priorities for living from three key Bible passages and evaluate how their personal priorities compare with his.

Bible Background: 1 Corinthians 9:19-27; Philippians 3:7-21; Hebrews 12:1-12

For Further Study: Read Chapter Four of *Claiming Your Place*.

PLAN ONE  Classes

BUILDING COMMUNITY

Write the following three topics on the chalkboard or a poster that you display as class members arrive:

If you had only twenty-four hours to live . . .

If you had $1 million you had to spend this month . . .

If you had to summarize your philosophy of life in ten words or less . . .

Give members sheets of paper and ask them to choose one of the topics to respond to. They should write at least two or three sentences on the topic of their choice.

After three minutes, each person should find someone else who made the same choice and share with each other what they've written.

After five minutes, discuss with the whole class: **"Was this an easy or a difficult assignment? Why? What do your answers say about your priorities for life? How can we tell a person's priorities? Is it easier or more difficult for the Christian to choose his priorities than it is for the non-Christian? Why?"**

"How can we know that a person's first priority is Christ?"

Write that question on the chalkboard and ask class members to answer it in one of these ways:

Discuss it with a neighbor for three minutes.

Write a paragraph to describe such a Christian.

Draw a picture or symbol to illustrate such a Christian life.

Write the summary of a book for its back cover that explains this kind of Christian. Choose the right title for the book and describe what it says.

After five minutes, let volunteers share what they've "created." Note similarities and differences between the ideas of your class members.

After using either or both of the above options, **tell the group that today's class session is about priorities. Choosing the right priority prepares a Christian to find his or her place in the church.**

OPTION
Instant Paragraphs
8–10 Minutes

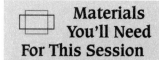

Materials You'll Need For This Session

Paper and pens or pencils, Resource Sheets 4A–4C

OPTION
Priorities and Possibilities
8–10 Minutes

CONSIDERING SCRIPTURE

**Bible Learning
Activities**
20–25 Minutes

First, we'll **look at how Paul expressed his priorities for living the Christian life.** Use one, two, or three of the following Bible-study options with your group:

OPTION
Marked Bible Passages

Distribute Resource Sheets 4A–4C, which contain the text of Philippians 3:7–21; 1 Corinthians 9:19–27; and Hebrews 12:1–12. Tell the class that the apostle Paul expresses the priorities of his life in these passages. (Note: The book of Hebrews does not mention Paul as its author, but many scholars attribute the book to him.)
Class members mark phrases in the passages:
circle = What the author says about his priorities.
* = How the author shows his priorities.
! = The author's encouragement for others to choose his priorities too.
Members should do this activity individually; then compare their marks with a neighbor and discuss the differences.

OPTION
List Paul's Thoughts

Divide your group into thirds. Each third studies one of the three Scriptures and makes three lists as if they are expressing the thoughts of Paul:
What I most want.
What I'm doing to demonstrate what I want.
My challenge to other Christians.
Give group members ten minutes to do their work. Then compare notes as the groups report to each other.

OPTION
Hymn Study

Students should read the three Scriptures (perhaps one-third of the class looks at each passage). Then group members look for hymns and choruses that express the commitment that Paul expresses and demonstrates in these passages.
After ten minutes, the groups suggest hymns and choruses to the whole class and explain how each one relates to Paul's priorities. Choose one of the hymns or choruses to sing together.

Summarize your discussion of these activities by challenging students to complete this open-ended sentence: "Paul's priority was. . . ." Write answers on the chalkboard.

CLAIMING YOUR PLACE

**Brainstorming
and Discussion**
10 Minutes

Tell class members that many people seeking a church home today do so with a "consumer mentality." That is, they choose a local congregation based on "What can the church do for me?"

Ask class members to brainstorm concerns and questions that might characterize such a mind-set.

Discuss, **"How does this approach contrast with the way Paul lived his life? Which attitude is closer to your own—the attitude characterized by the phrases on the chalkboard, or the attitude of Paul in today's Scriptures? Which attitude most helps a person find his place in a local congregation?"**

Ask the class, **"Which phrases or ideas from today's Scripture do you find most challenging? Which priority or passion of Paul would you most like for your own life?"**

Ask class members to return to their Bible-study groups for a prayer time as members respond to the last question above. You may want them to share their answers in this small group instead of with the whole class. After a brief discussion, members should pray for each other, asking God to help them discover their passion and choose the right priorities.

Closing Prayer
5 Minutes

PLAN TWO  **roups**

BUILDING COMMUNITY

1. *Tell the group,* Tonight we're going to be talking about passion. People have passion for many different things. Nolan Ryan has been known for his passion for pitching a baseball. Lee Iacocca is known for his passion for building cars and turning around Chrysler. *(Talk about people in your community who exhibit passion in what they do.)* What is something you've had a passion for?

2. *Option: Ask one or more of the questions under the first option in the Classes section on page 43.*

CONSIDERING SCRIPTURE

Read Colossians 3:1—4:6 (or have three people read 3:1–4; 3:9–17; and 3:23—4:6)

1. What words or phrases show Paul's passions or ambitions?

2. What things does Paul say should and shouldn't be our main ambitions in life?

3. What are the differences between a Christian's ambitions and those of an unbeliever?

4. Where does a Christian's passion come from?

5. What kinds of things should we do passionately?

6. Of the things we've just listed, which are easiest to do passion-ately? Which are hardest?

7. How does letting the Word of Christ dwell in us richly help us live the Christian life with passion?

8. How are devotion to prayer and living passionately for the Lord connected?

9. Most new Christians are filled with passion—for learning the

Accountability Partners

Have accountability partners do number 4 under "Claiming Your Place" together. Ask them to continue talking during the week and praying for one another.

OPTION
Worship Ideas

• Read Isaiah 40:28–31 together as an act of worship.

• Song suggestions
"Change My Heart, O, God," by Eddie Espinosa
"Refiner's Fire," by Brian Doerksen
"Ah, Lord God," by Kay Chance
"To Be Used of God," by Audrey Mieir

OPTION
Memory Verse

"Whatever you do, work at it with all your heart, as working for the Lord, not for men, since you know that you will receive an inheritance from the Lord as a reward. It is the Lord Christ you are serving" (Colossians 3:23, 24).

Word, for changing their attitudes and behaviors, for living for Jesus. But often, that passion fades in older Christians. Why do you think that happens?

10. Does passion have to fade the longer you're a Christian?

11. How can we keep our passion for Christ and his work alive?

CLAIMING YOUR PLACE

1. Many people today look for a church home with a consumer mind-set: "What's best for me and my family?" How is this mind-set different from the one Paul prescribes?

2. As we try to find our place of ministry in the church, how can Paul's teachings help?

3. Has God given you a vision for how he wants to use you in his church? What is it?

4. *Instruct participants to find a partner and discuss this question with each other.* Has your passion for living for Christ faded somewhat since becoming a Christian, or is it still strong?
• *Then have them pray for each other—for God to fill them with his vision and to give them strength and renewed passion.*

A MATTER OF *PRIORITIES*

1 Corinthians 9:19–27

19 Though I am free and belong to no man, I make myself a slave to everyone, to win as many as possible.

20 To the Jews I became like a Jew, to win the Jews. To those under the law I became like one under the law (though I myself am not under the law), so as to win those under the law.

21 To those not having the law I became like one not having the law (though I am not free from God's law but am under Christ's law), so as to win those not having the law.

22 To the weak I became weak, to win the weak. I have become all things to all men so that by all possible means I might save some.

23 I do all this for the sake of the gospel, that I may share in its blessings.

24 Do you not know that in a race all the runners run, but only one gets the prize? Run in such a way as to get the prize.

25 Everyone who competes in the games goes into strict training. They do it to get a crown that will not last; but we do it to get a crown that will last forever.

26 Therefore I do not run like a man running aimlessly; I do not fight like a man beating the air.

27 No, I beat my body and make it my slave so that after I have preached to others, I myself will not be disqualified for the prize.

Philippians 3:7–21

7 But whatever was to my profit I now consider loss for the sake of Christ.

8 What is more, I consider everything a loss compared to the surpassing greatness of knowing Christ Jesus my Lord, for whose sake I have lost all things. I consider them rubbish, that I may gain Christ

9 and be found in him, not having a righteousness of my own that comes from the law, but that which is through faith in Christ—the righteousness that comes from God and is by faith.

10 I want to know Christ and the power of his resurrection and the fellowship of sharing in his sufferings, becoming like him in his death,

11 and so, somehow, to attain to the resurrection from the dead.

12 Not that I have already obtained all this, or have already been made perfect, but I press on to take hold of that for which Christ Jesus took hold of me.

13 Brothers, I do not consider myself yet to have taken hold of it. But one thing I do: Forgetting what is behind and straining toward what is ahead,

14 I press on toward the goal to win the prize for which God has called me heavenward in Christ Jesus.

15 All of us who are mature should take such a view of things. And if on some point you think differently, that too God will make clear to you.

16 Only let us live up to what we have already attained.

17 Join with others in following my example, brothers, and take note of those who live according to the pattern we gave you.

18 For, as I have often told you before and now say again even with tears, many live as enemies of the cross of Christ.

19 Their destiny is destruction, their god is their stomach, and their glory is in their shame. Their mind is on earthly things.

20 But our citizenship is in heaven. And we eagerly await a Savior from there, the Lord Jesus Christ,

21 who, by the power that enables him to bring everything under his control, will transform our lowly bodies so that they will be like his glorious body.

Hebrews 12:1–12

¹ Therefore, since we are surrounded by such a great cloud of witnesses, let us throw off everything that hinders and the sin that so easily entangles, and let us run with perseverance the race marked out for us.

² Let us fix our eyes on Jesus, the author and perfecter of our faith, who for the joy set before him endured the cross, scorning its shame, and sat down at the right hand of the throne of God.

³ Consider him who endured such opposition from sinful men, so that you will not grow weary and lose heart.

⁴ In your struggle against sin, you have not yet resisted to the point of shedding your blood.

⁵ And you have forgotten that word of encouragement that addresses you as sons:

"My son, do not make light of the Lord's discipline, and do not lose heart when he rebukes you,

⁶ because the Lord disciplines those he loves, and he punishes everyone he accepts as a son."

⁷ Endure hardship as discipline; God is treating you as sons. For what son is not disciplined by his father?

⁸ If you are not disciplined (and everyone undergoes discipline), then you are illegitimate children and not true sons.

⁹ Moreover, we have all had human fathers who disciplined us and we respected them for it. How much more should we submit to the Father of our spirits and live!

¹⁰ Our fathers disciplined us for a little while as they thought best; but God disciplines us for our good,

that we may share in his holiness.

¹¹ No discipline seems pleasant at the time, but painful. Later on, however, it produces a harvest of righteousness and peace for those who have been trained by it.

¹² Therefore, strengthen your feeble arms and weak knees.

Five

Claiming a Place Full of Friends

I believe the best way to build up the body of Christ is through spiritual isometrics. The principle is seen in the exercise world and, surprisingly, the Bible. Strong, muscular bodies have reached peak condition because every part is tuned and pumped to the max. The same is true for the body of Christ. A preacher or dynamic staff can do a lot, but a church becomes dynamic when every member is tuned, functioning, and "pumped" spiritually.

An instructor at U.S. Total Fitness gym tells me that isometrics is a "workout with the body." There are no outside forces or machines.

The body parts, working together, tone one another!

When you, as a member of Christ's body, accept your connectedness to other members and interact spiritually, others are blessed by your efforts, and blessings also come to you. Your spiritual exercise of love stretches and strengthens you! It's called spiritual isometrics—"a workout within the body." —Tim Wallingford, *Claiming Your Place*

Central Theme:	We must make friends in order to find our place in the church.
Lesson Aim:	Students will discuss methods for making friends and biblical reasons for having and being a friend. Then they will commit themselves to using one of these methods in the next 30 days.
Bible Background:	Ecclesiastes 4:9-12; Proverbs 11:14; 12:15; 15:22; 24:6; 27:17
For Further Study:	Read Chapter Five of *Claiming Your Place*.

PLAN ONE  **C**lasses

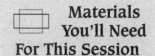
Materials You'll Need For This Session

Transparencies 5A and 5B, Resource Sheets 5A–5C, pens or pencils

BUILDING COMMUNITY

Display <u>Transparency 5A,</u> which contains a scrambled version of Ecclesiastes 4:9 from the *Living Bible.* **To begin today's session, challenge members to unscramble the verse: "Two can accomplish more than twice as much as one, for the results will be much better."**

Unscramble the Verse
5 Minutes

Ask the class to **name situations where they've seen the above verse true.** How many situations can they name in 90 seconds? Write them on your chalkboard or on a blank transparency as they shout them out.

Discuss: **"Have you ever needed a friend when you didn't have one? What did that feel like? Can someone who had that experience remind us of how important it is to have a friend?"** Allow time for several members to share.

Brainstorming
5 Minutes

Read, or ask a group member to read, the *Claiming Your Place* excerpt from page 53.

Tell the class, **"Today we'll look at the *value* of a Christian friend, and *how to get one.***

Read the Excerpt
3 Minutes

CONSIDERING SCRIPTURE

Choose one of the following Bible learning activities, or divide your class into groups and let each group choose one of the activities. (You may assign one of the activities to each group.) Or, if you have more time than the suggested twenty minutes, you may do these activities with your whole class, one after the other.

Bible Learning Activities
20 Minutes

Class members may use <u>Resource Sheet 5A</u> to study **Ecclesiastes 4:9-12.** This advice from Solomon contains several benefits of friendship. Members list these benefits on the sheet. Then, in the space provided, they should **draw an ad or write a radio or TV commercial "selling" the benefits of friendship.** They can do one commercial for their whole group or work alone. In either case, after about eight or ten minutes, they should be prepared to share their creation with the whole class.

OPTION
Create a Commercial

Class members may use <u>Resource Sheet 5B</u> to study **Proverbs 11:14; 12:15; 15:22; 24:6; and 27:17.** In *Claiming Your Place,* Tim Wallingford proposes the value of mentoring in building up the body of Christ. What do these verses say about the value of going to others for advice? In the space provided, class members list as many situations as they can in which a Christian will likely need advice in his lifetime. After working individually, the members should compare their lists with each other, in groups of two or three. Then they should circle the items on their lists that they've experienced. After several minutes, ask them to summarize for the whole class their conclusions about the need for mentors.

<u>Resource Sheet 5C</u> lists five ideas on "how to make friends." Members should read this advice, adapted from Tim Wallingford's chapter in *Claiming Your Place.* Then they should prepare at least three thirty- to sixty-second skits; each one should demonstrate one of these methods for friend-making. After about ten minutes, they should be ready to "perform" these simple skits for your whole group. Let the rest of the class see the list of ideas for making a friend and guess which method is being described by each skit.

If you would like to use these reproducible sheets, but don't want to use the methods they suggest, you **may simply make each of them the starting point for a small-group discussion.**

Divide your class into thirds, and each third into groups of between five and eight. Give each third of the class one of the resource sheets.

Those looking at Ecclesiastes can **list the benefits of friendship and discuss which benefit they have most experienced in their lives.**

Those looking at the verses from Proverbs can discuss, **"What is the value of going to others for advice? In which situations in your life have you most needed advice?"**

Those looking at the book excerpt can discuss, **"Which of these methods have you used most successfully? What happened? Which of these methods is newest to you? Would you try it?"**

FIND YOUR PLACE

Tim Wallingford suggests **three positive changes produced by Christian friendship:**

Character change. Both individuals grow in demonstration of the fruit of the spirit (Galatians 5:16-26).

Conversation change. Our conversational style becomes seasoned with salt and "helpful for building others up according to their needs" (Ephesians 4:29).

Commitment change. Our awareness of Christ's priorities for life begins to change our commitments. Our activities begin to fall more in line with what Christ would have us do. We become more willing to invest in the things that are truly important.

These are summarized by <u>Transparency 5B.</u> **Read the above quote,** and show each of the headings on the transparency as you explain it to your class.

Ask each class member to find a partner, or reassemble the Bible-study groups used above, to discuss: **"Which of these changes is most appealing to you? Which is most frightening?"**

Ask volunteers to share their answers with the whole group. Then send them back to their small groups to discuss, **"Which method for making a friend could you try this month? Which method could most help you find your place in the life of this congregation?"**

Commit to a Friend
5–10 Minutes

PLAN TWO  roups

PREMEETING

Before the meeting, make two signs. One says "Group A—Relational, Creative, Subjective Thinkers." The other says, "Group B—Content-oriented, Analytical, Objective Thinkers." Use as much creativity as you want in making these signs (or get one of your Group A people to do it beforehand). Place the two signs on opposite sides of the room, and, as people arrive, ask them to sit on the side that describes them the best. Group members may help one another decide. Be sure both groups have about the same number of people.

BUILDING COMMUNITY

Ask the whole group this ice-breaker question. What team or group were you a part of in junior high, and what role did you play?

CONSIDERING SCRIPTURE

1. *Use Resource Sheet 5D. Cut it in half along the dotted line and distribute the halves to the appropriate groups. In this Bible-study activity, Group A (relational, right-brain personalities) will read Ephesians 4:11–16 and answer left-brain type questions. Group B (analytical, left-brain personalities) will read Ecclesiastes 4:9–12 and answer right-brain type questions. The purpose of this activity is to show how working as a team with different types of people can be more productive. Do not tell the groups beforehand what the purpose of this activity is.*

2. *Option: If you want to keep the group together and use a purely discussion format, use Resource Sheet 5D to guide a discussion of each of the two parts of the study. Watch who answers which questions and how individuals respond to the questions. Then go to questions six and seven below.*

3. *After the groups have finished, come back together and ask each group to summarize what they discussed.*

4. *Ask Group A how they felt answering these "touchy-feely"*

Materials You'll Need For This Session

Resource Sheet 5D, pens or pencils

Accountability Partners

Ask accountability partners to meet at the end of the meeting to talk about how their friendship is growing. Ask them to encourage each other in how their friendships are helping them claim their places of service in the church.

OPTION
Worship Ideas

• Read Proverbs 27:2, 5, 6, 9, 10, and 17; and then pray, thanking God for the blessings of friends.

• Song suggestions "Bind Us Together," by Bob Gillman "We're a City Not Forsaken," by Celia Cross "In Christ There Is No East or West," by John Oxenham

OPTION
Memory Verse

"Two are better than one, because they have a good return for their work: If one falls down, his friend can help him up. But pity the man who falls and has no one to help him up!" (Ecclesiastes 4:9, 10).

---

questions. Ask Group B how they felt answering these analytical questions. Did they feel any frustration doing this activity?

5. Do you think you would have been more or less productive if we had mixed the types of personalities into both groups?

6. From both texts we studied, what are some benefits of teamwork in the church?

7. How can you tell if a congregation—or any group within it—is working as a team or not?

CLAIMING YOUR PLACE

Pick a function you would like to concentrate on as a group. Here are a few ideas: supporting each other more, reaching out to non-Christian friends and neighbors and inviting them to the group, doing a service project together, including worship in meetings. Ask the group, **How can we use all our different gifts, abilities, and interests as a team to _____?** *Ask the creative people in the group to brainstorm ideas. Ask the analytical people to figure out how to put them into practice.*

Who Needs a Friend?

Solomon's advice in Ecclesiastes 4:9–12 lists several benefits of friendship. Write them here. Then draw an advertisement or write a radio or TV commercial "selling" the benefits of friendship. Be prepared to share your creation with the whole class.

Which benefit of friendship have you most experienced in your life?

Guess Who Needs Advice!

Being a member of Christ's body automatically means "connectedness." Paul makes this point very clear when he says the whole body is "joined and held together by every supporting ligament" (Ephesians 4:16).

Paul adds in the same verse that spiritual isometrics is the best way to tone up the body parts for maximum result! He says the whole body "builds itself up in love, as each part does its work."

Webster defines *mentor* as one who is a "loyal friend and a wise advisor."

Solomon says, "Wise advice satisfies like a good meal" (Proverbs 18:20, *The Living Bible*). Everybody needs, from time to time, good advice and a loyal friend.

—Tim Wallingford, *Claiming Your Place*

Read Proverbs 11:14; 12:15; 15:22; 24:6; and 27:17. Then, in the space below, list as many situations as you can in which a Christian will likely need advice in his lifetime. After you've made your list, compare it with another's. Then circle those situations that you've already experienced.

What is the value of going to others for advice?

When have you most needed advice in your lifetime?

How to Make Friends

• *Pray for a friend.* Ask God to help you be friendly and to send a friend your way.

• *Get involved in a group.* A Sunday school class or house fellowship provides opportunities to meet new people.

• *Get involved in the church.* God provides Christian friends through ministry. The apostle Paul made most of his close friends this way. A modern ministry example is teaching. Suppose you teach a children's class. By your ministry, you put yourself in a position to meet people and, therefore, make new friends. As you attend teacher meetings, call parents on behalf of the children, and serve with your co-teachers, you will be in contact with potential friends.

• *Make friends through mutual needs.* A group of Christian moms called POPS (Parents of Preschoolers) meets on a regular basis. Through a common need and interest, they come together to sharpen one another more effectively in parenting as Christian mothers.

• *Encourage one another.* Several years ago a Christian man ran for public office and lost. He was devastated. I had the opportunity to encourage John through his time of disappointment and personal setback. We would jog and end up at a donut shop for a Coke or a cup of hot chocolate. When the crisis passed, we continued to jog, share the Lord, and pray for one another. Our families took trips and worked together in the youth ministry. I have since moved to another ministry location, but our friendship continues.

Act it Out!

Choose at least three of the above methods for making a friend. For each one prepare a 30- to 60-second skit to illustrate how a Christian would use this method to make a friend.

Which of these friend-making methods have worked for you?

Which is the newest idea?

Will you try it?

Group A

Read Ephesians 4:11–16, and then answer the questions below.

1. What is the purpose of the leadership positions mentioned in verse 11?

2. What are the results of gifted people working together?

3. What do you think the "supporting ligaments" of the church are?

4. Summarize this passage in twenty words or less.

- -

Group B

Read Ecclesiastes 4:9–12, and then answer the questions below.

1. Is it easy or difficult for you to ask someone else to "help pick you up"?

2. How important is it to you to have a Christian friend who can pick you up or keep you warm . . .

    . . . emotionally?

    . . . spiritually?

3. How do these verses make you feel about the importance of friendships?

BETTER WILL
THE BE TWO
TWICE ONE
FOR MUCH
ACCOMPLISH
AS RESULTS
MORE THAN
MUCH CAN AS

Christian Friendship
PRODUCES THREE POSITIVE CHANGES . . .

✗ Character Change

✗✗ Conversation Change

✗✗✗ Commitment Change

Six

Claiming a Place of Flexibility and Change

*I*t seems strange to be making a biblical case for flexibility and change, but claiming your place in the church requires adaptability. Your attitude toward change will have a big impact on your personal growth. Flexible people are growing people. Growing people make for growing churches. . . .

Finding and claiming your place in the church is a continuing process of change. Not all change produces growth, but all growth means change. Godly change is achieved by allowing biblical principles to rule our lives. Christians and churches who know and apply the Bible, who live by faith, and who follow godly leaders are typically growing Christians and churches.

The place God wants each of us to find is the place that allows us to change until we conform to the likeness of his Son. Have you found your place? Are you willing to change to find it?

—Myke Templeton, *Claiming Your Place*

Central Theme: A Christian must embrace change in order to find his place in the church.

Lesson Aim: Group members will look at the reality and necessity of change, consider Scriptural admonitions to change, and decide how they may need to change in order to find their places in the church.

Bible Background: Matthew 18:3; Romans 6:4; 7:6; Ephesians 4:22–24; 2 Corinthians 5:17

For Further Study: Read Chapter Six of *Claiming Your Place.*

PLAN ONE  **Classes**

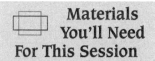 **Materials You'll Need For This Session**

Poster board, Resource Sheets 6A–6C, pens or pencils, Transparency 6A

BUILDING COMMUNITY

Write this question on your chalkboard for members to see as they arrive: **"How is your life different today from the way it was ten years ago?"**

Ask them to think of at least six answers to the question. Then each member should find a partner and share his list of changes. After five minutes, let a few share their answers with the whole class.

OPTION
Listing
5 Minutes

Write this sentence on a poster that you display as class members arrive:

**"Although not all change is growth,
all growth is change.
To grow, then,
we must be willing to change."**

Divide the class into groups of between three and five members each. Ask each group to think of examples to prove this statement true: physically, emotionally, and spiritually. Give them five minutes to discuss. Then ask several to share with the whole class. Discuss with them, "How have you seen this true in your family, in your work, or in the church?

OPTION
Evaluate the Quote
5–7 Minutes

Use both of the above discussion starters. Divide your class into groups of three. Half of the groups discuss the first question. The rest of the groups discuss the second question.

OPTION
Half and Half
10 Minutes

As a transition into Bible study, discuss with your group:
   1. How should we feel about change?
   2. Can you remember a change that you at first dreaded or resisted but now can see that it turned out for good?
   3. What makes change sometimes difficult or unpleasant?
Tell your group that the premise of today's study is that **growing churches are changing churches. And to find our place in such a church, we must be willing to welcome change in our own lives.** Today's discussion focuses on why this is true, and how to make it happen.

All-Class Discussion
5 Minutes

Considering Scripture

Letter-Writing
10–15 Minutes

Distribute Resource Sheet 6A, titled **"How Does God Feel About Change?"** It leads students to read the following verses and write a "letter to Christians at the end of the twentieth century," expressing what they believe to be God's point-of-view on this issue. The suggested verses are Matthew 18:3; Romans 6:4; 7:6; Ephesians 4:22–24; 2 Corinthians 5:17.

Read and React
10 Minutes

Resource Sheet 6B contains a brief excerpt from *Claiming Your Place* titled, "Godly Change Requires Godly Values." Distribute it to the class and ask members to read it and then discuss, **"How do we know when to change and when to resist change?"** They should jot down two or three principles in the margins of their handout.

Option
Half and Half
15 Minutes

Perhaps you will want to **distribute both handouts** to the whole class. Let members decide which assignment they want to work on. Students should work in groups to complete one assignment or the other. Then let groups share their conclusions with the whole class.

Claiming Your Place

Option
Consider the Checklist
10 Minutes

Resource Sheet 6C contains a checklist of changes from *Claiming Your Place*. Each one has been experienced at the congregation where writer Myke Templeton ministers. **Distribute the checklist to class members and challenge them to decide how they feel about each one. Which changes would be difficult for them to accept in their own church?**

Option
A Change Continuum
10–15 Minutes

Ask class members to **jot down, on a scrap of paper, the names of five Christians they know.** These should include a cross section of church members: perhaps a leader, a staff minister, a fellow Sunday school class member, a family member, etc. At the bottom of the list they should write their own name.

Display Transparency 6A. which shows a range of reactions that may be demonstrated toward change. The numbers one through five are used to indicate some of these different reactions.

For each name on their list, members should put one of these numbers to **indicate that person's attitude toward change.**

Members need not tell what numbers they put beside each name, but discuss with the class: **"What insights on the issue of change does this exercise give you? Which is easier, to talk about change, or actually to change? Suppose you could be convinced that a change in your life or in some programming or procedure** at church would result in leading several people to Christ and heaven. Would you be willing to endure the change in order to achieve that result?"

After either of the above activities, lead a guided prayer time: **"God, help us see your will as we contemplate changes in our lives. . . ."**

Groups

BUILDING COMMUNITY

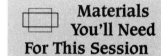
Materials You'll Need For This Session

Index cards, pens or pencils, Resource Sheet 6C (optional)

Distribute index cards and make sure everyone has a pen or pencil. Ask the following questions, giving participants time to answer each one on their cards. Tell the group not to share their answers out loud.

1. If you could choose any other first name for yourself, what would it be?
2. If you could change careers without any financial concerns, what would you do?
3. If you could change anything about our church (or this group), what would it be?

After everyone is finished, have them fold their cards in half and place them in a bag or basket. Then ask each person to take one card. (It's OK if they get their own.) On the backs of the cards, they should write, down the left side, numbers for each person in attendance. For example, if there are eight people in attendance, each person will write 1–8 down the left side of his or her card.

Go around the circle and have each person read the responses on the card he or she is holding. Give time for each person to guess "whose card is this?" on the back of his or her card. After going completely around the circle, have everyone, beginning with number one, reveal his or her identity. Then see who got the most guesses correct.

Option: What is the biggest change you've made in your lifetime?

CONSIDERING SCRIPTURE

Today, we're looking at how flexibility and change impact the growth of the church and individual Christians. The book of Acts records change after change as the church grew. We'll look at a few of these changes now.

Pick several of the verses listed below to study. The bold-faced passages are recommended as first choices. You may divide your large group into several smaller groups, which will study individual passages. Or, especially in a smaller group, study a few of these passages together.

OPTION
Accountability Partners

Have partners meet and discuss all three questions under "Claiming Your Place." Ask them to encourage one another in the positive changes they've already noticed, especially since this series began.

OPTION
Worship Ideas

• Read Psalm 46 together as an act of worship.

• Song suggestions "Change My Heart, O God," by Eddie Espinosa "God Is My Refuge," by Judy Horner Montemayor "Have Thine Own Way, Lord," by Adelaide A. Pollard

OPTION
Memory Verse

"We will not all sleep, but we will all be changed— in a flash, in the twinkling of an eye, at the last trumpet" (1 Corinthians 15:51, 52).

Here are some of the passages to chooses from:
Acts 1:6–11; 2:1–4; 2:37–39; 2:42–47; 4:5–22; 6:1–7; 8:2, 3; 9:1–31; 10:9–16; 10:23–48; 16:6–10
Ask the following discussion questions.

1. What changes in **attitudes** do you see in these passages?

2. How do these changes help individuals or the church to grow?

3. Do you see any resistance to change in these passages?

4. What results from this resistance?

5. How difficult do you think it was for these people to change how they had always thought or how they had always done things?

6. What gave these people the courage to face change?

7. What do you think of this statement: "Christians are called to be change agents"?

8. *Option: Distribute Resource Sheet 6C.* Check the items that would make you feel uncomfortable. *Then discuss these with the group.*

9. What impact does your attitude toward change have on . . .
   . . . your spiritual growth?
   . . . the growth of the church?

10. Change often produces anxiety. How can you learn to deal effectively with change?

CLAIMING YOUR PLACE

1. To become the person God wants you to be, what changes do you think you personally need to make?

2. How can this group help each other make the changes we need to make?

3. What changes in our congregation (or in this group) do you need to accept?

How Does God Feel About
CHANGE?

The following verses give us a clue to how God feels about change: Matthew 18:3; Romans 6:4; 7:6; Ephesians 4:22–24; and 2 Corinthians 5:17. Read each verse, and then use the space below to summarize God's perspective on the subject. Write a "letter to Christians at the end of the twentieth century" that tells what you think God would say about this difficult issue.

Dear Christian,

With love,
Your Heavenly Father

GODLY CHANGE REQUIRES GODLY VALUES

For us to mature into the men and women God wants us to be, we must learn to value the things that matter most to God. Three priorities have a large impact on the church and the Christian desiring to grow.

The Word of God—Years ago I came across a little rhyme that has helped me a great deal in ministry:

> Methods are changing,
> Principles never do;
> Methods are many,
> Principles are few.

Anytime we talk about change, we should also talk about things that should never change. Foundational teachings of Scripture and the doctrines of God are the anchors of our faith. They are nonnegotiable. These are things we would be willing to die for. They do not change.

However, methods of doing ministry are always changing and need to change if we will ever successfully carry out our mission.

A church is always outgrowing programs and events because, like people, healthy churches grow. In fact, if something isn't growing, something is wrong with it, and it won't be long until it starts to die.

Faith—"Then he touched their eyes and said, 'According to your faith will it be done to you'" (Matthew 9:29). To me this verse means you expect great things from God. You allow room for God to work.

The Bible is full of stories that show how vital faith is to our daily walk with him. For example, Exodus tells how the Israelites had their backs against the sea while Pharaoh's army was closing in on them from the front. Their choices were simple: die by drowning or die by the dagger. Then Moses answered the people, "Do not be afraid. Stand firm and you will see the deliverance the Lord will bring you today. The Egyptians you see today you will never see again" (Exodus 14:13).

Faith gave them the strength to experience the great change God had in store for them. It will do the same for us.

Leadership—There is a high level of trust in the leadership of our church, but trust doesn't happen overnight. It takes years to develop, and it is not the result of a single decision. It is the result of a process. Leaders gain trust the old-fashioned way—they earn it. How? By setting visionary budgets, initiating new programs, hiring good staff, standing firm on important issues, being benevolent yet assertive.

Trust is earned by putting together a portfolio of spiritual success and attaining worthwhile goals.

 **Checklist**

Which items on this list would make you uncomfortable? Why?

- ❏ Size of the facility increases several times
- ❏ Continual building programs
- ❏ Relocation project
- ❏ An increasing diversity of people
- ❏ Style of worship changes
- ❏ Music style changes
- ❏ Style of preaching changes
- ❏ Increase in the number of programs
- ❏ An increasing number of people attending
- ❏ Not able to see the preacher on a regular basis
- ❏ More accountability with offerings
- ❏ Increase in the number of ushers and servers
- ❏ Increase in the expense of maintenance
- ❏ More frequent stewardship campaigns
- ❏ More people wanting to become members
- ❏ An increasing need for several evangelism programs
- ❏ People will die and be buried without the preacher's knowledge
- ❏ Increase in the number of worship services
- ❏ Fewer announcements from the pulpit
- ❏ Increase in staff size
- ❏ Inability of preacher to make all the hospital visits
- ❏ Staff not available as much
- ❏ Loss of anonymity
- ❏ People sit in "my" seat
- ❏ No place to park
- ❏ Walk a long way to get to church
- ❏ You feel your complaint doesn't seem to matter as much
- ❏ You don't recognize anybody sitting around you
- ❏ The Sunday school class is growing larger
- ❏ "I don't feel like I fit in"
- ❏ "Nobody appreciates my past accomplishments"
- ❏ "I have to give up my classroom"
- ❏ Everything has to be cleared on the calendar
- ❏ The preacher spends more time with new people than with the old people

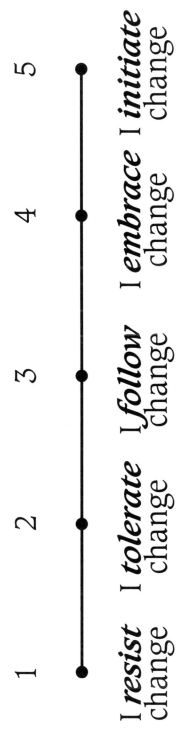

1 2 3 4 5

I *resist* change

I *tolerate* change

I *follow* change

I *embrace* change

I *initiate* change

Seven

Claiming a Place of Extravagant Action

W hat is the vital nugget of truth Jesus wants us to hear, to see, to learn? Put simply, he wants us to do something—something he can call beautiful, something from the heart. He wants us to love him before anything else. He wants us to do whatever we can in his name—without caution, without mathematical calculation, but in an unbridled, abandoned extravagance. No reserve. Nothing withheld. Nothing saved back. He wants the last drop of our resources to be lavished on him.

One man has said that "a certain excessiveness is an important ingredient of greatness." By that measure, Mary was truly great. And by Jesus' own testimony, her unbridled extravagance will never be forgotten.

—Steve Wyatt, *Claiming Your Place*

Central Theme: We will most likely claim our place in the church if we will simply choose some service and begin doing it right away!

Lesson Aim: Members will list how Mary's extravagant action of anointing Jesus can be a model for our service to him today.

Bible Background: Matthew 26:6-13; Mark 14:1-9; and John 12:1-8

For Further Study: Read Chapter Seven of *Claiming Your Place*.

Classes

BUILDING COMMUNITY

Display again the posters from session one with the titles from all the sessions in this study. Tell the class, **"These discussions have laid before you some heavy challenges. Which session has been the most challenging for you?"** Perhaps students should share in pairs before you discuss with the whole class.

Ask, **"What have you decided so far about how to find your place in the local church? Whose responsibility does it seem to be to help you find your place? What kinds of sacrifices and commitments are required of the person who finally finds his place?"**

Tell the class that this final session is no less challenging, but the action-oriented members may find it most satisfying. **Today's study looks at an example of one person who did what she could for Jesus, without waiting for permission, at some personal risk. Perhaps some class members will decide that her example can spur them on to find their place in the church.**

CONSIDERING SCRIPTURE

Ask three different volunteers to read aloud; each volunteer reads the account of the anointing of Jesus from a different Gospel record: Matthew 26:6–13; Mark 14:1–9; or John 12:1–8.

Divide the class into groups of between five and eight, and ask them to **analyze the story by using the three discussion questions on Transparency 7A.** You may decide to display the questions for members to see as they're listening to the readings of the story.

Distribute Resource Sheets 7A and 7B. They contain quotes from the last chapter of *Claiming Your Place* and discussion questions after each one. Ask a class member to read Matthew 26:6-13 aloud before members look at the quotes and discuss the questions. They may want to refer to the passage as they discuss. Divide the class into groups of between five and eight. Assign one of the quotes to each group, so that every quote is discussed. If a group has time after they've discussed their assigned quote, they

All-Class Discussion
8 Minutes

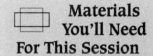
Materials You'll Need For This Session

Posters from session one, Resource Sheets 7A–7C, Transparency Master 7A, pens or pencils

OPTION
Analyze the Story
10 Minutes

OPTION
Quotes and Questions
20 Minutes

may move to any other one they choose. After five or six minutes, discuss the quotes with the whole class.

CLAIMING YOUR PLACE

Session Summary
10 Minutes

Look again at the titles from the seven sessions in this study. (If you made posters for the first session and kept them till now, display them in your classroom before class members arrive.) Ask a volunteer to summarize each session. (A different volunteer should summarize each one.) Ask, **"Which of these steps toward claiming your place have you already taken? Which are you still pondering? Which do you feel you may never take?"**

OPTION
Listing
10 Minutes

Use the above three discussion questions, but in a different way. Distribute blank sheets of paper to your class members. Ask them to make three lists, one for each of the questions. Or ask them to arrange the seven titles in order, from "The step I'm most likely to take" to "The step I'm least likely to take."

Give them five minutes or less to write. Then let volunteers share some of what they've written.

OPTION
Strategy Writing
10 Minutes

Distribute Resource Sheet 7C. Ask class members to **list their strategies for claiming their places in the life of the church.** Their summaries should reflect their responses to the discussions in this course.

Those who wish may share with the whole class what they've written.

Sentence Prayers
5 Minutes

Close with a time of sentence prayers, reflecting on this closing discussion. Encourage members to express their commitments to God aloud.

Groups

BUILDING COMMUNITY

1. What three things have you spent the most amount of money on?

2. If you had one week to live and you had to spend all of your $500,000 in savings before you died (or your money would go to the government), what would you do?

3. *(For a group of couples)* If your spouse had only two weeks to live, what would you do for him or her? How much would be too much to spend?

CONSIDERING SCRIPTURE

Read Mark 14:1–9. *(Leader, also read Matthew 26:6–13; Luke 10:38–42; and John 12:1–8 before the meeting as background for this study.)*

1. Why do you think the woman "wasted" more than a year's wages on something that would last only a few minutes?

2. Why were the disciples so indignant?

3. How do you think you would have reacted if you had witnessed this scene?

4. How do you think you would have reacted if you were the breadwinner in this woman's family?

5. What were the woman's priorities as opposed to the others who were there?

6. Jesus called what the woman did "beautiful" because it came from a heart of love and devotion to him. What beautiful things have you seen done by Christians, either for you or someone else?

OPTION
Accountability Partners
Direct accountability partners to discuss how each is putting into practice what he or she has learned in this series. Have both partners found and claimed a place in the church? Ask them to pray for each other's ministries and daily walk with Christ.

OPTION
Worship Ideas
• Read Psalm 115 together as an act of worship.

• Song suggestions
"I Love You, Lord,"
by Laurie Klein
"Father, I Adore You,"
by Terrye Collho
"With All My Heart,"
by Babbie Mason
"Take My Life and Let It Be,"
by Frances R. Havergal

OPTION
Memory Verse
"So whether you eat or drink or whatever you do, do it all for the glory of God"
(1 Corinthians 10:31).

CLAIMING YOUR PLACE

1. The woman served Jesus despite what others thought and any consequences she might suffer. Is there anything you've ever wanted to do to serve others or worship Jesus, but you were afraid of what others might think or something that might happen?

2. Jesus said, "She did what she could." Jesus doesn't expect us to do what we can't do. He wants us to use the gifts he's given us to do what we can. What are some of the things he has given you gifts to do for him?

3. Jesus said the woman's act would be remembered wherever the gospel is preached throughout the world. We are living the fulfillment of that prophesy now! What do you think you'll be remembered for?

4. Have you ever sensed God calling you to do something for him, like starting a new ministry or going a new direction in your life?

5. What is your next step in claiming your place in the church?

6. *Have group members pair up with one another to discuss what steps each one needs to take to get involved in the ministry of the church or to put more passion into what he or she is already doing.*

7. *Suggest that several members get involved in the same ministries together. They can team up to serve, supporting and encouraging each other as they do.*

" ? " ? " ? " ? " Quotes and Questions

The following quotes are from Steve Wyatt's chapter in *Claiming Your Place*. First read Matthew 26:6–13. Then consider these comments that arise from that story. After each one, discuss the accompanying questions with a friend.

Are you willing to do something God calls beautiful? Is your church willing to successfully do something God calls beautiful?

When Jesus called Mary's actions "beautiful," he used the word *kalos,* which, in its larger meaning, infers giving life to the lifeless. It carries with it the difference between my attempt to paint by numbers and a true artist who can make an image literally leap from the canvas. It's the difference between someone who can sing the right notes and blow the right tune and another person who can take that same collection of notations and make chills run up your spine.

True beauty lies far beyond the numbers. It's much, much more than just the notes. And it's certainly not, "What's it going to cost?" or, "How much time will it take?" Rather, it is, "How much of myself am I willing to invest?"

Have you seen someone do something for God that qualifies as beautiful by this definition? What did it look like? When have you been motivated to invest yourself for God, rather than simply do a job in the church? What would motivate you to that level of commitment again?

Jesus said, "When she poured this perfume on my body, she did it to prepare me for burial" (Matthew 26:12). Understanding that the time was short, Mary seized the moment. That's why Jesus said what he did about the poor in verse 11. He wasn't putting down ministry to the poor. He was just saying that the time for such acts of love was short. The moment would never pass their way again.

Can you think of a situation when timing was crucial to make Christian service effective? Have you ever seen an opportunity for God lost because someone hesitated or waited?

According to Mark's record, Jesus said, "She did what she could" (Mark 14:8). That's what Jesus wants. He doesn't expect you to do what you can't! Only what you can. You don't have the wherewithal to feed the whole world, but you can feed one person. You cannot comfort all who are weary, but you can comfort one or two. You can't change a whole generation of young people, but you can teach one Sunday school class and flow into their lives with the love of Jesus. . . .

Most of us are waiting to win the *Reader's Digest* sweepstakes before we give as we've always wanted to give. Some preachers are waiting to serve a big church, and then they'll preach as they know they can preach.

Why wait? Don't sit around dreaming about giving what you don't have; give what you do have. Don't just sit around wishing you had more time to be involved; invest the time you do have. The fragrance that honors the Lord is not a book filled with wishes, but a life emptied in service.

Why is it easier to dream about what you'd like to do than actually to do something now? Have you ever known someone who constantly talked about what he or she was going to accomplish some day? What can we do to keep ourselves from being like that person? Can you do the things mentioned above? What else could you do?

Most folks don't understand extravagance. They think you're showing off. Mary dealt with that all her life. Her sister Martha criticized her for not helping out in the kitchen because Mary just couldn't pull herself away from Jesus. And even the disciples scolded her for what they considered a lavish, unnecessary deed.

But Mary was just emptying her heart. She didn't even consider what others would think. Their praise was the last thing on her mind. She was in love with Jesus, so in love she couldn't *not* do what she did. The love of God gripped her heart, and she acted.

How might fear of criticism keep some Christians from trying something extravagant for God? How might it be possible to do something big for him without seeming to show off? How might fear of criticism be an excuse for inaction rather than a good reason?

Have you ever been criticized for trying something too big for God? If not, is it possible this is a sign you haven't gone far enough in your service?

My Strategy
for Claiming My Place
in the Life of the Church

A MODEL OF *Extravagant* ACTION

1. What did Mary do that could be called extravagant?

2. What risks did Mary take? Why would common sense have told her to hold back? Why do you think she was so bold?

3. What "rewards" did Mary receive for her action? How do the results of her extravagance affect your willingness to try something big for God?

OTHER *CREATIVE GROUPS GUIDES*
from Standard Publishing

11-40306
(ISBN 0-7847-0286-1)

Hearing God
Guide by Michael C. Mack and Mark A. Taylor
Help your group or class learn how to read God's Word—and really understand it! In just six lessons, you will demonstrate eight simple steps that can make anyone feel at home in the Bible. Use this resource to help your class or group learn to . . .
- Get Ready for Bible Study
- Read So They Know What the Bible Means
- Look at the Big Picture
- Make Sure Everything Is in Place
- Look at Topics, Customs, and Styles
- Put Their Bible Study Into Practice

To order, contact your local Christian bookstore, or call toll free
1-800-543-1353

STANDARD PUBLISHING
Cincinnati, Ohio

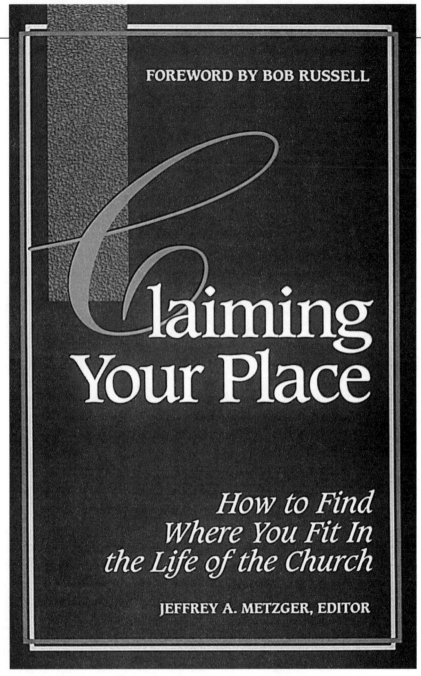

FOREWORD BY BOB RUSSELL

Claiming Your Place

*How to Find
Where You Fit In
the Life of the Church*

JEFFREY A. METZGER, EDITOR

To purchase a copy of
Claiming Your Place,
edited by Jeffrey A. Metzger,
contact your local
Christian bookstore or
call Standard Publishing toll free

1-800-543-1353

11-40304 *(ISBN 0-7847-0284-5)*